BARTERNOMICS

How to fund your business start up, business overhead, business expansion, or your next vacation without money!

Learn how to stop paying for everything
and still get what you want

By Debbie Sardone

BARTERNOMICS

Debbie Sardone
3634 Long Prairie Road, Ste. 108-214
Flower Mound, Texas 75022
www.thebarternomicsbook.com

ISBN 978-0-692-01212-3

Dedication

This book is dedicated to my late father-in-law, Ron Sardone, who gave me the confidence to become an entrepreneur. And to my husband Steve for encouraging me to pursue my dreams and never give up, standing by me every step of the way, for over 33 years.

Table of Contents

Introduction

1. Barter Grows On Trees
2. Rescued By Barter
3. Barter Economics
4. Barter Is Booming
5. Love Thy Barter
6. Keeping It Legal
7. Save Your Cash
8. Dollars And Sense
9. Making Money With Barter
10. Barter Smarter
11. Manage Barter Better
12. Barter Is A Guaranteed Sales
13. Employee Benefits On Barter
14. Like Wonder Bread
15. Nothing To Barter?
16. Barter For Start-Ups
17. Let's Make a Deal!
18. Say "I Do!" To Barter
19. The Perils And Pitfalls Of Barter

Lessons From My Barter Broker
Resources
About the Author

Introduction

Starting a maid service out of the trunk of my car, I surprised my family and peers when we quickly grew to a million-dollar-a-year operation. I didn't know at the time that I had achieved something extraordinary, later learning that only about 2% of the maid services in the United States ever reach a million dollars in annualized sales. I just assumed all the cleaning services out there were bigger than me—not! But then, not long after the events of September 11, 2001, I found myself wondering if I would go out of business after nearly 20 years of astonishing success and prosperity. The heartache and disappointment of watching my sales steadily drop with the spiraling North Texas economy, was nothing compared to the endless sleepless nights produced by worry and fear. How was I going to meet payroll? How do I afford the increasing insurance premiums? Who else can I lay-off in the office? How will I pay the 941 tax and the sales tax this month when they're both coming due in the same week? Believing I was experiencing just a temporary economic "hiccup" rather than an economic crisis, led me to put miscellaneous business expenses on my credit card to preserve that precious cash for taxes, rent, payroll, and other necessities. I saw credit card debt as a simple solution to a "short term" problem. I had no idea that "short term" would become a 3 ½ year mess. Expenses were rising, customers were quitting service or cutting back frequency, and my credit card balance was reaching terrifying levels. If only I'd known then what I know now....hind sight is 20/20. I am a problem-solver by nature. Give me a challenge and I'm all over it. Give me an obstacle and I'm energized by working on a way through it. I'm not a quitter—never have been. I am a tenacious problem solver.

But my plummeting sales nearly drove me to business despair. Oh the humiliation of riches to rags, if I couldn't turn things around. The budget of my million dollar enterprise kept pressing down on my tiny little shoulders. But the music in my head "....I will survive....." was louder than my creditors, and I did. Now we're stronger than ever, and a healthier company for it. So how did I turn things around, and even grow 10 years later, during the "worst economy" our nation has seen in decades (the recession of 2008-2009)? Well, I believe the answer is simple (not to be mistaken with "easy"). Defeat is NOT an option for me. It's never been a part of my vocabulary. Every failure is an opportunity for improvement, which leads to success. Failure is simply *success delayed.* This is not business psychobabble, it is the driving principle I live my life by: in marriage, in parenting, in business, in life. So if defeat is not an option then finding a solution is the only option. "Learning" to barter was one of the first steps I took towards turning my business around and I've never been the same since. Hmmm......"all things work together for good......".

Barter Grows On Trees

Money doesn't grow on trees, but barter does. Plant the seeds, water the soil, pay close attention and barter bucks will sprout all over the place. Learning this brilliant business concept helped me pay my bills when cash was tight (or non-existent) which enabled me to stop running up so much credit card debt.

I had Lasik eye surgery last year and didn't pay a dime for it. Instead, I plucked some money off the "barter tree" and made my appointment with the doctor. If that sounds too good to be true, you're reading the right book!

I'd wanted Lasik Surgery for several years. I'd reached that stage of life where I needed reading glasses and they were scattered everywhere, at home, in the office and in the car, but naturally I could never find a pair when I needed them. Then, there was the cost...$1,100 or more per eye for the surgery. Somehow, the frustration of groping for a pair of reading glasses was more tolerable than the thought of the cash outlay.

One day I got an email from my "barter broker" that my barter association had just signed on a new "trade member"—a Lasik surgeon in the Dallas area!

The doctor listed had performed over 50,000 of the surgeries and came highly recommended from local acquaintances outside the trade association. Once I met him, I felt very secure about his technical abilities and confident he and I would be a good fit for my needs.

Quite honestly, what floored me was that I could barter with a doctor. Thousands of business men and women, regardless of their industry or the color of their collar, are bartering with one another because they have discovered the power of barter in today's economy. Whether you are trying to rescue your business, launch a start up, improve your bottom line, or fund your "fun", read on to see what barter can do for you.

Rescued By Barter

How well I remember the prosperity days of the late 80's and 90's- a time when business was booming. When I started my business 29 years ago times were good. We had more clients than we knew what to do with and our phones rang off the wall with the smallest amount of advertising. Clients were asking for weekly and bi-weekly cleanings and we kept a two week waiting list of people willing to take last-minute appointments if we got a cancellation.

That was the good news. The bad news was the country was experiencing the worst labor shortage in its history. Every business in town had a large sign or banner, "NOW HIRING," and each prospective employee we interviewed expected more benefits and bonuses than the last but only wanted to work a little bit. We secretly knew customers were "a dime a dozen" but a good employee was worth their weight in gold.

Despite it all, we grew like crazy. We treated every client like our first and provided our "cleaning techs" with good, sound training and worked to inspire loyalty and provide stability for them, for us and for our clients. Each dollar of profit was valued, and every business expenditure agonized over.

Hindsight being 20/20, I look back at all those cash expenditures and shake my head. If only I'd understood the value of barter. Back then, barter never entered my mind, in fact, it wasn't until I'd been in business another 12 years and was struggling through a severe recession, that I realized the miracle of barter economics.

My epiphany came a few years into our economic decline, when everyone was on edge and business had stalled-out. I had eliminated all the non-essentials and, to cut costs even more, moved my business across town to a low-rent district. We were literally hanging on for dear life. I didn't have the cash to buy the phone system we needed for the new office and I did not want to put another $5,000 on my business credit card. We had to leave the old system in the office we moved from since the circuit board was outdated and not portable.

Like many business owners, I was trying to solve a classic business dilemma with traditional business logic. We had to have an updated phone system but we didn't have the money to buy it. The 'Ah Hah!' moment came when a persistent "barter broker" (that had tried unsuccessfully in the past to sign me on as a new "trade member"), kept tossing out suggestions of how I could "spend my barter". He always said "spend your trade, save your cash", but I didn't really grasp the concept. I had resisted his offer to join the trade group numerous times arguing that "I need money, not stuff!". Whenever he'd call on me he would list a few things I could be getting on trade: "mailing lists, dental work, car washes, signage, a new phone system.......". "Whoa—back up, what did you say?" I was finally paying attention instead of waiting for an opportunity to interrupt and tell him once again, "no thank you". You mean I could trade cleaning services for a phone system? It suddenly made perfect sense. I had been focused on what it would *cost* me to barter instead of focused on the *savings* and the *guaranteed sale* that barter provides for those "must have" expenditures. I signed up that day, and I've been bartering ever since.

Barter Economics

It's sometimes referred to as the 'mother of all economic concepts,'—but I call it BARTERNOMICS. Barter predates money. People have exchanged what they've had in hand for what they needed since time began. Inland folks traded meat and crops for coastal fish, weavers traded with furriers. Today, even kids trade carrot sticks for cupcakes. No money? No problem. But don't let an old concept fool you into thinking it's outdated and no longer relevant. To the contrary; barter is more valuable today than ever before. With the convenience of the internet, I trade goods and services from literally all over the world. My options are broader than ever. I've bartered for 30,000 brochures that shipped from China, I've sold consulting time to clients 10 states over, and I've vacationed in another country, all on barter.

Barter is easy and, in the midst of the 2001 recession, it was the 'hand-up' my business needed. I didn't have the money to give employee raises or spend on advertising, let alone that phone system we desperately needed. Whether you are struggling to pay your business expenses, as I was, or you want to expand without incurring debt, you'll discover barter is an essential tool to building your bottom line.

From the beginning, bartering has most commonly been done privately and directly between two individuals. I offer to clean your office; you agree to do my bookkeeping. It's all about trading services or goods rather than buying them with money. The hardest part in private barter relationships is finding people to agree to barter with you and then staying "even" on expenses.

Knowing the people and businesses with whom you trade is certainly helpful to satisfactory private barter, but clearly communicating the specifics of your trade is absolutely essential. Put all the details of services, values and timeframes in writing and consider the particulars of how to redeem trade values if one of the businesses falters. Private barter can be time consuming because it requires careful management. This is why I lean heavily on conducting all my trade through a formal trade association. It's safe, easy, and legal.

Early on, I exchanged (as a private barter) house cleaning services with a local yellow page publisher. I needed advertising; he wanted his offices clean and neat. We struck the deal with hope and a handshake.

But, by the time I realized it, I had provided his business with over $4,500 worth of cleanings yet I had only received $1,100 worth of advertising. To add insult to injury, he sold his business before I received the balance of the advertising owed me and never did recover the outstanding $2,400 in trade.

TIP: When it comes to specifying the terms of a trade, a handshake is not enough. Treat barter exchanges like cash transactions and put your agreements in writing!

The best kept business secret is bartering through third-party trade associations. They're organized solely to broaden and manage your barter while eliminating the common risks associated with private barter. Such barter businesses, often called "barter exchanges", "trade associations" and "barter groups", provide members with a larger marketplace of goods and services and management of all barter transactions, utilizing an online "barter bank account". The fees are minimal so the benefits far out-weigh the cost.

There are advantages to trading both privately and through an organized network. Both enable business owners to give and receive without paying cash, and both require setting the rules of exchange. But, whereas private barter between one business and another demands the business owners track what they receive and resolve any differences themselves, organized barter businesses handle those management headaches and even help identify new barter business opportunities for their members who are in need of any good or service.

While my business can only provide residential and commercial cleaning services locally, the national trade association to which I belong credits me for those cleanings and those credits are available for me to spend throughout the barter network nationwide, from legal services out of Lexington to business coaching out of Baltimore to a vacation week in St. Thomas.

Did I realize this when I was cash-poor and credit-strapped? Not at first. Then, thanks to that persistent "barter broker", I finally got it—barter was not just the ONLY option during those tough financial times, but the *best* option for the future as well. If you have surplus time or product, you should be bartering it and racking up the "spending credits" or "barter bucks". Period. I signed up to barter, started cleaning "on trade" and bought my new phone system with my barter credits. I was on a roll—what else did I need? By the way, I used my lowest paid, "staff-in-training" to do the work. The work was still guaranteed, the girls were still well-trained and carefully screened and supervised, like they would be on any "cash-paying" job. I saved my "seasoned" staff for my "cash clients" of course. "Cash" in the world of barter simply means a non-barter client, whether they pay by cash, check, or credit. The bartered cleanings were still top-notch and good practice for my "Rookies". Everyone was happy. And since Tele-Zone was professional and courteous throughout the entire phone system installation, I felt comfortable referring him for "cash" business to others.

> TIP: The word "cash" in the world of barter means any sale that is not on barter. So a "cash" client is someone who pays with check, credit card, or cash, rather than barter. "Cash" in the barter world is non-barter payment in any form. Of course, cash is king!

For my first trade, my barter association broker introduced me to the other barter member whose business was phone systems and installation, making initial introductions smooth and easy. The owner came out and installed a full PBX phone system with all the lines and stations we needed. He customized the system to our needs, trained us on the system, and treated us like his favorite client, yet not a dime would change hands! He utilized used phone systems from his "cash" jobs when clients upgraded. He cleaned, repaired and tested those phones, offered them on barter, and then installed them himself to avoid paying one of his employees to do the work. The out of pocket expense for him, was zero, so the $5,000 trade credit he got from the job was worth the one-day investment of his time and a few follow up training appointments. I think he said he was saving up trade credits to take his wife on a luxurious vacation...........A barter 'bankroll' beats spending cash or buying on credit any day!

Barter Is Booming

By now I hope you see that **Barternomics** is not an outdated concept. Barter is big business and booming. According to Reuters, an estimated 250,000 North American companies were actively engaged in barter transactions worth an estimated $20 billion in 2009. During the first half of 2009 alone, North American barter companies reported increases between 15 and 35 percent in transaction values. Corporations like Southwest Airlines and American Express barter. Craigslist recently reported an increase of 125 percent of bartered goods and services. The tougher the times, the more people recognize barter as a "solution" rather than as an "expense".

Worldwide, the barter exchange and trade industry, both private and organized, is said to have grown to more than $20 billion from multi-national corporations to mom-and-pops exchanging goods and services. Both the Internet and sophisticated relational database software programs have further advanced the barter industry's growth here and abroad. It's no surprise, this 'cashless' economy is gaining momentum, not losing it.

For years, I traded straight up with my hair dresser, a monthly haircut and color (a $120 service) for a monthly house cleaning (a $120 cleaning). It was simple. But, when my hairdresser had her baby, she wanted bi-weekly service. Balancing her cleaning needs with my hair needs became more difficult and becoming "upside down" in the trade credits was virtually impossible to avoid. Private trades like these are a natural part of doing business locally. They make sense and help you build your business in the community (women know that a hairdresser in a high-end salon TALKS and this "trade partner" has referred many "cash customers" to us). On the other hand, tracking trades on your own requires time and attention, so relationships aren't negatively impacted. So, private barter beware. It's also a legal transaction that the IRS views the same as "cash", and therefore a taxable event. You have to be diligent about tracking those transactions in your books to avoid a tax penalty if discovered through an audit.

TIP: Never underestimate the value of personal referrals. Bartering is a powerful way to develop business relationships that raise awareness about you and what you do.

While I still do some local, private bartering, I prefer to do as much barter as I can through the organized barter groups because the advantages and reduced risk is worth the minimal expense (cash fees).

Membership in organized barter groups comes with a broker; someone who gets to know you and your business, and who will help you maximize the benefits. In fact, a good broker will help you create a demand for your business within the organization, to get you accruing trade credits or increase them.

Membership fees in these organizations are usually modest and are sometimes waived or discounted if you refer another business owner who joins as well. Each group is different, but most follow a similar structure.

Barter organizations consider it their business not only to track and manage the accounting of all the goods and services exchanged among members, but to do so smoothly and efficiently, keeping everything legal with the IRS. Your account is available online 24/7 and your broker (usually the one that signed you up locally) is there to facilitate all trade relationships.

"Debbie, you'll be trading $20,000 in services a year, before long," Gary Smith, my ITEX Trade Exchange Broker told me when I first joined the barter group. I didn't believe him but within two years of joining I was actively 'buying and selling' in the organization to the tune of thousands of dollars, trading my cleaning services for goods and services I had previously purchased with credit or scarce cash. And, the more I saw available in the barter marketplace, the more motivated I was by the cashless opportunities. My goal quickly became to *never pay cash* until I first checked to see if I could buy it on barter!

Of course, your business cannot survive without "cash" paying customers, but I learned quickly my business could avoid BEING a "cash" paying customer (remember, the definition of "cash" in the world of barter is a non-barter payment of either check, credit card payment or the ever-disappearing cash payment—it's not a literal term of green paper bills).

Love Thy Barter

Ahhhhh, I love barter. Paul Doumeng owns a beautiful, all-inclusive resort called Bolongo Bay, on an island far away from Texas. Now, of course my maid service is located north of Dallas. Because we are both members of the same trade exchange, we each got what we wanted without spending a dime.

Paul needed to remodel the resort. He needed thousands of dollars worth of new mattresses, furniture, lighting, fixtures and island décor for the hotel rooms, lobby and restaurants. Paul 'sold' $30,000 worth of vacation packages to people in the barter group using that barter credit to 'buy' everything he needed from various vendors in the barter group.

I used barter credits I had accrued to buy that romantic vacation package for my husband, Steve, and myself. A waterfront room, fantastic meals, sunset sailboat cruises and long afternoons lounging on the beach under the palm trees, in the U.S. Virgin Islands. Bolongo Bay Resort was one of the nicest vacations I've had in years. They accrued credits from all of us, enabling Paul to revamp the Resort using his barter credits to make his acquisitions cash- and credit-free. Does a cashless economy sound better and better to you and your business?

Keep in mind I'll never clean Paul Doumeng's house or the resort he operates in St. Thomas. But I will be providing bi-weekly cleaning services to *someone* in the trade exchange group who lives in my area, for about a year, to accumulate the barter credit I used up, on this "business-trip". You see, I used that trip to write BARTERNOMICS and turned it into a legitimate business expense, fully tax deductible!

It was such a wonderful experience, I've told everyone about our stay at the Bolongo Bay Resort. And I certainly hope Paul gets some "cash customers" from the rave reviews. To their credit and, in keeping with the professionalism you want in a barter organization, the owners of Bolongo Bay Resort never treated us any differently than their cash customers. We felt special from the moment we arrived: they never singled us out for less than their best treatment or services, just because we were there on barter. Sadly, not all businesses in the barter exchanges ascribe to this ethical practice. We also dined on barter at 'The Room With A View', an upscale restaurant, in downtown St. Thomas. Again, another delightful experience, royal treatment, a seat by the window, and an exquisite meal all paid for with my barter credits.

Organized barter groups give you the opportunity to trade for more goods and services than you could ever dream of getting through private barter while keeping everything safe and legal. I prefer to do all my trading through the association and even try to convert my private barter clients and friends to the organized group.

Keeping it Legal

Now, if you're starting to think barter is a great way to avoid taxes, you would be wrong. Cashless does not mean tax-less. There are no tax advantages (or disadvantages) to bartering. Uncle Sam views barter transactions as cash, and he expects his share of the deal. Whether you are bartering for business or personal reasons, informally or through a trade association, keep careful track of the trade value of your exchanges because they are subject to taxes. If you're the type of business owner that buries personal expenditures inside your books as business expenses, then I suspect you'll do the same with barter, but you are risking the same threat of discovery by the IRS if audited.

Barter is a sale and, therefore, a taxable event like any cash sale. If you would normally charge sales tax, then your barters are taxable, but it is customary to collect the sales tax in cash and barter the rest. Now on the upside, whether business *purchases* are made with cash or through barter, they are all considered business expenses and, as such, are fully tax-deductible. Keep barter purchases even with barter sales and the transactions will be a "wash", producing no "profit" that would be taxed.

It's just smart to avoid creating a taxable event, by making business purchases with your business barter credits. For example, when I sell $300 worth of housecleaning, I purchase $300 worth of business products or services, like printing, advertising or copy supplies. I don't go and get pampered at spas or salons in the barter group. If I did, the $300 barter expense would not be a legitimate business expense and would not create a "wash" for the barter sale. If you plan it right, keeping barter sales and purchases even inside a fiscal year, you will never pay income tax on business barter. Keeping an accurate accounting is essential and therefore making organized trade exchanges all the more desirable, worth every penny of the small transaction fees charged.

Bartering through a trade association means the association handles all the accounting. In fact, the associations are required to issue a Form 1099-B of members' annual transaction value to the IRS on your behalf. All barter proceeds are reportable as income – one barter dollar equal to one U.S. dollar – and must be included on your federal income tax return. But, remember, your barter purchases for business expenses will, be fully deductible.

Private barter also requires reporting transactions as if they are cash income, based on the fair market value of the goods and services traded. So, for example, if you are a printer and print marketing materials for an attorney, in exchange for legal services, both businesses need to report as income the fair market value of the goods and services exchanged, with business-related transactions being deductible. Of course, in private barter, reporting is rare, conducting those barters "under the table". This is risky, just like burying non-business expenses in the books. If you are audited and discovered, you'll pay hefty fines.

So, be very clear: Bartering business services for personal 'purchases' will create a taxable event for your business. There's nothing wrong with that of course, but be sure and set aside the taxes you'll owe on the "profit". If I barter $300 worth of cleaning for $300 worth of tanning, the tanning is not a business expense and won't offset the barter 'income' of the maid service "sale". There is nothing wrong with mixing business and personal barter, as long as you are aware the value of the personal services received will not qualify as a tax-deductible business expense. Unless, of course, you are a swimsuit model and need that tan for a photo-shoot!

Bartering for personal services, house cleanings, haircuts, dental services, babysitters, dry cleaning, travel (for pleasure), health clubs, restaurants and the like is treated no differently by the IRS than any other non-business expense. Barter transactions for personal use are considered as cash income for tax purposes. Plan for it, or just use your barter for legitimate business and don't worry about it.

I know a photographer who does a lot of barter. He is brilliant at capturing special occasions, weddings, family reunions and the like. And he likes to exchange his professional services for a variety of needs, both business and personal. He photographed a friend's wedding in exchange for a year of lawn services for his home. He also photographed a 50th Anniversary party in exchange for a year's worth of oil changes for his car. He was smart enough to know that the personal service he received in exchange for his photography (the lawn service) was considered income but was not a deductible expense on his tax return; therefore, he paid income tax on that bartered "sale". The oil changes, however, were a legitimate business expense since he uses his car for business. He put aside enough money to cover the taxes on the lawn care trade, while enjoying the savings on the oil changes as a business expense.

The bottom line is this – when you barter, keep careful track of your transactions. When you're bartering for business, make sure you spend your barter dollars as they within your fiscal year, and when bartering for personal services, put away enough money to cover any taxes owed.

Save Your Cash

Business owners know it's all about keeping the green stuff—the cold, hard cash. Every business owner learns it's easier to spend money than to make it. My barter practice is simple: never turn down cash customers - those who are ready, willing and able to pay for my goods and services. Alternately, never pay cash yourself for business expenses if you can find someone else who will barter with you. Sometimes this means changing vendors to do so. Save your cash: barter instead. This mindset will help you build your business and bankroll all your cash. I've switched printers several times to do business with one that will barter, rather than just give me a discount as a loyal "cash" customer.

I look for every opportunity to barter these days, and you should, too, whether you own a business or not. For example, my office lease does not include pest control service or a security alarm system, so I trade with each of these service providers, saving that monthly cash outlay. In Texas, if you don't want to see roaches in the office you pay for monthly pest control. And the peace of mind that comes from having our offices monitored by a security alarm company is worth the minimal barter expense.

In most cases, if you've been someone's paying customer, your service provider may not want to barter if it means losing your cash, anymore than you want to lose theirs. The point is to begin looking for every opportunity to barter for your business' needs, even if you have to switch vendors. Another way to talk a "cash" vendor into bartering with you is to upgrade on barter. That's what I did with a publication in which I'd advertised for some time. I'd been paying $200 a month for advertising and when I asked the Account Rep about bartering instead, she said they weren't willing to lose the cash. I don't blame her, I wouldn't either—but it never hurts to ask.

What she couldn't pass up, though, was my offer to upgrade my ad to a larger size,--something I couldn't afford anyway. I paid cash for the original size and bartered the difference between the larger ad. Also, in another publication, where I had not been a cash customer, I was able to do full barter for remnant (unsold) space throughout the publication. We created a drawing-style give-away worth $1,200 to her readers in ads that featured my company. I got far more than $1,200 worth of ad space, and she got to offer a cool "sweepstakes" type program to increase loyalty and exposure for her publication. My out of pocket expense would only be about $600 in labor and materials on the $1200 give-away when the drawing was held. The remnant space I received cost her nothing to give me, yet that additional exposure for us was priceless and provided my business with thousands of dollars worth of high-end ad space I could not have afforded otherwise. We both win.

Using barter instead of cash makes sense in other ways. Take the purchase power of your cash, for example. Every dollar you receive is deflated by the costs of overhead, materials and labor. Yet barter is straight dollar-for-dollar value. Take a look:

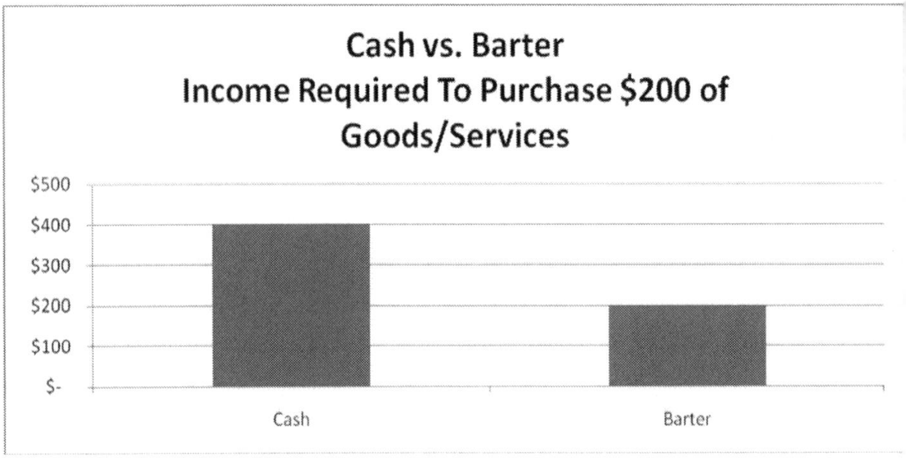

It takes me $400 in cash sales to end up with $200 of actual purchase power, because of the "cost of goods sold" factor—which is 50% for me. Ouch! In other words, Every time I sell $400 worth of cleaning $200 comes right off the top to pay my labor—and I haven't even added the payroll taxes yet! So to pay for a $200 "cash" ad I have to sell at least $400 worth of cleaning (but actually more, since I have not calculated payroll taxes, supplies, overhead, etc.!)

With barter, your purchasing power is equal to the size of the sale. This is never the case with cash-based transactions. If I barter for a $200 ad in your publication, I only have to give $200

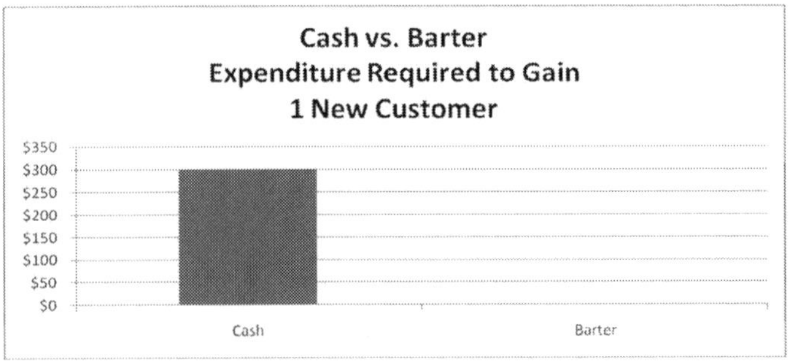

worth of cleaning, not $400. Another benefit of barter is you have NO marketing costs to obtain that "barter client". This is a huge savings, one most people don't even recognize. Although every industry is a little different, marketing is a factor in all of them, to attract and establish new customers. With barter, there are NO marketing costs and yet you benefit from the referral of those with whom you trade. See below:

It costs me approximately $150 in advertising alone to obtain one new (cash) client. My labor alone (not including payroll taxes, materials, overhead, or administrative costs) are approximately 50% of the sale. Therefore consider the following:

If I owe $200 to the printer for stationery and business cards, I will have to sell more than $550 worth of cleaning to pay for it (because I paid $150 in advertising to find that new client-sale, and then my 50% labor costs come off the top, before any profit is available to purchase with).

If I traded $200 worth of cleaning straight up for the $200 in printing, I come out ahead. First there was no initial customer acquisition cost (the $150 I have to spend to obtain a new client). The only cost is my labor and payroll taxes (which on a $200 job will cost me about $110. Barter isn't free, but it is cheap. It only cost me $110 for the printing, paid for with just a $200 barter sale, vs. a $400 cash sale needed if I paid with cash. And the broker fees are only a tad higher than the "merchant fees" when my cash clients pay by credit card.

Dollars And Sense

A friend of mine has a handsome collage in his office, right over his desk. It's the 57 credit cards he and his wife amassed during their 'glory days.' They had a credit card for every store imaginable, at the time when charging purchases wasn't just easier, it was essential...no one carried cash. When the couple's financial bubble burst and they set about digging their way out of debt, they cut up all of the cards, making a vivid, gilt-framed reminder of the destructive power of credit.

Even if you were one of the smart ones who avoided the credit card crunch, our economy's sensitivity to world affairs and its recent freefall, have radically changed the way most of us look at our finances. Business spending is no different. Having cash in the bank automatically reduces your vulnerability in a tight economy or emergency situations, while it increases your power to seize new opportunities when they arise. The most reliable cash-preservation tool I know is barter.

Let's compare traditional business purchases with barter. Formerly, when I made buying decisions, I knew I would have to generate more than twice the new expense in revenue to cover my costs (labor, materials and overhead) and pay for the new expense. So, as I stated before if I purchase $200 worth of advertising, I will have to generate more than $400 in cleaning sales to cover the cost of the ads I purchased. I also have no guarantee of earning the revenue necessary for both because the expense will be due no matter how successful the marketing is. Making the purchase in the "cash" world does not guarantee the sales to pay the bill when it comes due.

Of course it was tempting to pay cash (when I had it) or, possibly, put it on credit, but either way, I bought "worry", never knowing if my new expense would pay for itself, let alone increase sales, which was the point anyway.

Let's look at this same situation with barter. If I want to add $200 a month of new advertising and can barter, I provide the publication or publisher with $200 worth of cleaning services per month and they provide me with $200 worth of monthly advertising.

Bartering <u>cuts</u> my out-of-pocket expenses to just $100, my direct cost before payroll taxes, for a $200 cleaning, if my margins are 50%. By bartering, I don't have to put up $200 of my cash for advertising OR worry who is going to schedule $400 of cleanings to cover my advertising 'investment' and business costs. Even more important, that advertiser was NOT coming through my door as a paying customer anyway; so they weren't banking my money, just hoping for it. Barter is a guaranteed sale.

Barter works because you get what you need from someone who wasn't going to pay you with cash in the first place but who is willing to guarantee you goods or services of equal value to yours.

'Cash is King' only when it comes 'IN' your door. The next time a vendor "just stops by," talk trade options and see if he or she has something of value to trade. Discuss trading the fair market value of your well-respected goods and services for his or hers. If they say "yes" you just made a guaranteed sale that will pay your next business expense, keeping cold hard-to-come-by cash in the bank.

If he or she wasn't signing on to become your new, best-paying client, turning the transaction into a trade is the next best thing. It's not better than cash, it's better than "no thank you, I can't afford your service". And, when you're scouting your next business purchase, whether it's a marketing campaign, logo shirts for the staff, an updated phone system or pest control, hang on to your cash and use your head. Barter makes perfect cents.

Making Money With Barter

My absolute favorite reason to barter is you can actually make cash money from it. It's true - I've received a ton of cash business by using my barter and, if you're creative, you too can increase cash sales by bartering.

One way to 'cash in' is to offer eye-catching specials to fill your slow days (months or seasons?) or unload surplus inventory.

Take Mondays, one of our slower days in the maid service industry, and many other industries as well. When we have eight open appointment slots on a Monday, I'll send out an email the Friday before to prospects or "one-time" clients, offering them a deal they simply can't refuse. One of the campaigns that works well for us reads, "*Schedule maid service for Monday and get A Maid, A Merlot, and A Massage!—first come, first served. Call now, only 5 available!*" My phones light up like a Christmas tree! The complimentary bottle of merlot was obtained on barter, as was the $65 massage. When I have restaurant certificates on barter, the campaign offers "A Maid, A Merlot, and A Meal!" Instead of offering a "$25 off coupon" in the ad, reducing the precious cash paid by the customer, I offer a $65 massage that carries a high perceived value, but will only cost me $35 in cleaning labor and it's a more appealing "sell" than a coupon, insuring a scramble to buy from me! I've used other bartered items as give-away's in my ad campaigns like oil changes and sporting event tickets at Father's Day, as well as tickets to the circus and Disney On Ice for more general purpose campaigns. Almost all of the goodies I offer are things I've gotten through barter, reducing my cost factor to about half. I bartered for ten cases of wine, paying (trade dollars) $40 and $50 for some bottles, $12 to $15 for others. (I have to say, my husband and I kept the "fancy" wines; and use the less expensive bottles, for my giveaways!)

My "*Schedule regular maid service and get a candle light Dinner for Two*" ad campaign is also made easy with barter, using restaurant gift certificates obtained on trade. A $25 gift certificate to a favorite, local Italian restaurant costs me about $13 when I do the cleaning. The $12 bottles of wine cost me $6 or $7 when I do the cleaning. No cash was used, no credit card debit incurred, only the bartered sale that will be redeemed later by cleaning for the goods, and the high-perceived value of these give-aways generates multiple "cash" sales for my light days that would have gone unfilled.

Adding value to your normal goods or services is a great way to incentivize people to try you for the first time. When you get those items through barter, you can give away more for much less. We typically sell at least three or four $120 to $300 cleanings from these last minute promotions, time that would not have been sold anyway. And, it often leads to sign up for repeat service, which is what we are really striving for in the first place. Barter enables me to offer creative little incentives to "go ahead and try my service". What started out as my inventory of bartered goodies turns into business I didn't' have on the books 12 to 24 hours earlier, potentially creating a reliable, cash-paying customer who will spend about $2,600 a year with us if they go with bi-weekly.

Ive made thousands and thousands of dollars with email campaigns like these, selling my light days, last minute. It only takes a little thought and creativity. In fact, I teach an entire course on creating email campaigns that GET NOTICED, not deleted, and using bartered items is a big part of implementing my course.

Use your database to target promotional campaigns to one or more groups of customers, prospects and "one-timers," Select your bartered items for give-aways, based on whose attention you want to grab and what's on peoples' minds. Like Father's Day = oil changes or full service car wash and detail (obtained on barter of course). Mother's Day = this one's easy, massages, 4 hours of child care, dinner for two, facials, there's tons of barter for the moms!

One of my all-time, most successful promotional offers was a "*Back to School*" special. The first day of school I sent out an email promo for "A Maid, a Massage, and a Merlot," available with one of our "Spring Cleanings," a Top-to-Bottom deluxe cleaning that typically starts at $300 and goes up. We sold over $2,000 worth of services for what was otherwise a 'light day' on our schedule! Our employees had work, our bottom line was dramatically improved and the massage gift card and wine were all from.......well you know where they came from!

Creatively packaging what you already sell, using bartered items, can have a surprising effect on sales. One holiday season, we wanted to break all records for the cleaning industry by selling *thousands of dollars* in maid service gift cards instead of the usual *few hundred dollars worth.* We promoted our biggest maid service gift card offer ever - resulting in our largest gift card sales ever. I simply packaged up 12 months of maid service and included $200 worth of high-perceived value items for free--

items I obtained through barter. So, instead of simply offering the usual $100 and $200 Maid Service Gift Cards for the holidays, I put together the 'Ultimate Holiday Gift for Someone Special' campaign, promoting "Maid Service for a Year - Both Practical and Romantic!" We wrapped up twelve of our $100 maid service gift cards in a large, beautiful gift basket, filled with bartered goodies: a gift card for a massage, a bottle of wine, wine glasses, and a restaurant gift certificate. We tossed in elegant, individually wrapped chocolates, a few pretty candles from the dollar store, wrapped the entire basket in cellophane and put a pretty bow on the top. They sold like hot cakes, to the tune of $12,000 in November and December, solving the shopping dilemma for the guys, and delighting spouses on Christmas Day with a year of freedom from housework. A win-win for us all. And the "freebies" included were obtained on barter.

This campaign was so popular, we had one wife call up and say, "*My husband wants to talk to you about your maid service for a year gift card basket...here he is, hold on.*" The husband got on the phone, sounding a little bewildered; he asked if this would make his wife happy this year. Without missing a beat, I assured him it would, "putting her in a good mood every single month for the next twelve months!" He whipped out his credit card and started reading off the numbers. It was the free massages and the merlot that enticed him to go ahead and "spoil" her for a year with this special gift. Barter just makes sound business-sense every way you look at it.

Barter Smarter

Anyone with a product or service can barter. Some companies are better suited to barter than others, because of their margins, unsold surpluses, or their high capacity structure. But, whatever your business, you too can have a powerful and lucrative experience with barter. You just have to give it a try and keep trying until you find the right mix.

Consider accounting, business coaching and consulting, cleaning, lawn service, legal counsel, maintenance, marketing, media production, painting, plumbing, printing, and telemarketing; these businesses are prime candidates for bartering and all found in barter associations.

Auto lettering, auto service and repairs, carpet cleaning, computers, computer service, computer training, dentists, direct mail, graphic design, hair stylists, salons and spas, magazine advertising, massage, 'music on hold' creation, office equipment, office furniture, office space, PBX systems, pest control, pool services, promotional products, radio and TV advertising, rental equipment, rental facilities, restaurants, security systems, sign makers, sporting events, tanning salons, vacations, web design, and web hosting—just to name a few. All necessary goods and services businesses routinely use and have traditionally paid cash for. STOP it! These businesses and many more are ideal barter partners and want to trade with you.

Companies with high capacity, slow days, or excess time make exceptional barter collaborators. Airlines, concert venues, restaurants, hotels and stadiums can all count on empty seats, tables, or rooms that eat up overhead without generating income. When offered on barter, they fill empty seats or rooms with customers who will buy sodas, hot dogs, promotional products, dinners, or other services, as well as adding cash revenue for parking or alcohol sales, etc. The added sales can even exceed the bartered seat (or room). How is that not a cash-cow for venue-sellers, hotels, and transportation merchants? Not to mention the gratuities (which is always in "cash" and never bartered) for employees that otherwise would have gone without on those light days. Likewise, the media - TV and radio stations, magazines, newspapers, and direct mail – are likely traders, as they invariably have 'remnant' ad space and air time to fill.

On the other hand, if you sell custom-order, high-dollar materials with narrow margins, very specialized equipment, or goods that require significant up-front, out-of-pocket costs to produce, barter may set you back more than you will recoup in an exchange. While charitable contributions of such goods may, on occasion, bring you acclaim or recognition for your specialty, such goods do not always lend themselves to routine barter, that is unless you can expect a high percentage of conversions to additional, long-term repeat business as a cash transaction. In that case, the barter is like the "loss-leader" and well worth it. An example of this might be a printer who only offers to print expensive portfolio folders only one time on barter, but unlimited barter on brochures, stationery, and business cards. The business cards, stationery, and brochures are cheap for him to offer on barter since it's usually done "in house", the portfolios might be costly to him to offer, but he hopes you re-order them every few months on a cash basis, thereafter, especially since he already has all your artwork files and it's convenient to deal with the printer who does your business cards. Another way a business can create a long term cash customer from a barter relation is using this scenario: Say a nail salon only offers your first full set of acrylic nails on barter and all pedicures on barter. The follow up bi-weekly nail "fills" are not offered on barter, but on a cash basis only. The barter-er can get her first full set of nails on barter (usually more expensive than "fills") and can come in for her pedicures on barter. But, since she's already there, she's more likely to go ahead and pay cash for the "fills" too, every other week for years. That's turning a bartered service you don't sell enough of (the pedicures) into a cash-cow for your core business (filling acrylic nails twice a month for life). This is a smart use of barter.

The majority of us, will find our business products and services are, in fact, perfect for barter. That being said, there are a few "tricks of the trade" essentials to maximizing your barters.

First, smart barter is intended to keep you from paying cash. Always try to barter for those things you can trade instead of paying cash. Remember this barter mantra: cash IN, barter OUT. We want to acquire as many "cash" clients as we can, and we want to buy as much on barter as we can. These are two different groups of people and rarely one and the same. Never, ever invite a cash-paying client to become a barter client. You've just lost precious cash if you do. The only time you would barter with a cash client is for additional products or services they will not buy from you. For example, I would not offer a bi-weekly cash-paying client to barter with me. But, if they had something I need (like printing), I might offer to start cleaning for them on a *weekly* basis and only barter those extra cleanings they weren't buying from me in the first place.

Second, smart barter means being prudent about what you are willing to trade and when. Select wisely from among the variety of goods and services you provide. My screen printer, embroidery service is always willing to barter for white T-shirts and logo golf shirts, but she won't trade specialty items she has to special order and pay too much for (like jackets, ball caps, and tote bags). Her margins are too low on those items, and so it's not worth her time and out of pocket expense to do on barter. But, because I buy logo shirts from her, and my logo is already digitized, she gets my cash business when I do need those type items.

Third is timing. Selecting wisely is also about when your goods and services will be available for trade. I don't barter Thursday or Friday cleanings. The cost of cleanings on these days is no different than Monday, Tuesday, or Wednesday cleanings, but I have no trouble getting cash paying customers (thankfully) who will do anything for a clean house just before the weekend. I'm not filling those premium spots with barter clients, I reserve the "light days" for them. Likewise, accountants may be very willing to trade services all year but won't take you on in March or April. Once you're a barter client though, they won't leave you hanging; they'll work you in before the 15th, or at least file an extension so they can wrap up your job after the rush.

Fourth, keep exchanges even. It is important that both parties in a barter relationship agree at the outset to a fair and even exchange. That doesn't mean your services are priced equally, it just means you agree that for every $500 spent with you, you'll get $500 to spend as well. So, if you're an attorney bartering with me, you might create my family will for $1,000 of barter, and I have to give you $1,000 worth of house cleaning.

We held our employee dinner and awards banquet at a local Italian restaurant for two years in a row on barter. We got $1,200 worth of food, facilities, and beverage for 30 employees and their spouses and the restaurant owner gave his wife maid service for a year.

Fourth, for the sake of the transaction and your business reputation, define the barter and use contracts if you normally would. The relationship should not be based on "a handshake" contract just because it's barter. Anything can go wrong. Issue your normal "satisfaction guarantee" and treat the barter just like any other cash customer.

Manage Barter Better

Managing your barter business effectively means embracing three fundamental principles.

1. Limit barter transactions from 5% to 20% of your total sales volume.
2. Apply the "Golden Rule" to barter clients as you would for cash clients: "Do unto others as you would have them do unto you." In other words treat them with equal respect, fair pricing, and enthusiasm, the way you hope to be treated when you redeem your barter bucks.
3. Clearly articulate your barter terms, limitations, conditions, or guarantees, right up front.

Barter is big because it preserves in-coming cash and enables you to buy things you couldn't otherwise afford or for which you wouldn't shell out cash money. However, trading too much can jeopardize your profit margins, especially if you're buying too many things you would otherwise do without. It's not "free money" so don't waste it on stuff you don't need. I recently ordered dozens of coffee mugs with my company logo on them to give away at networking events, to guests that visit my office, or VIP customers. It's a little luxury I've always wanted, but just could not bring myself to shell out $500 cash since money has been so tight. So when I saw logo mugs were available on barter I jumped at the chance and ordered several dozen. And, since we make up those lovely gift baskets with the wine and a couple of toasting glasses ($1 glasses from Sam's Club or the Dollar Store) I had the logo vendor put our company name on a couple dozen wine glasses too. Looks really special in the gift baskets, all on barter. It's an affordable way to look even more professional—an investment in my image, and well worth it. But, I've also purchased things on barter that had a short expiration date and watched them expire, wasting money. This is a careless use of barter and eats into the savings created.

Because James Cash Penney understood that one single dissatisfied customer is more powerful than 99 satisfied customers, The Golden Rule became his business's guiding principle. Even today, more than 100 years later, that's the way J.C. Penney is still run. You, too, will find treating cash and cashless customers with equal respect and attention pays big dividends to the value and respect your business builds.

Barter clients, like cash clients, can be a great source of referrals for you. Believe me – I have seen both sides of this. I have been treated so badly by a barter vendor that I would never in a million years choose to do business with them again, let alone refer my "cash" clients, family or friends to them. This usually happens with a barter member who inflates his pricing because it's barter.

I'm a promoter. I want my business and yours to succeed. Give me knock-your-socks-off service in a barter situation, and I will let everyone know, just like I do for cash services. Treat me as if you're doing me a favor or can't be bothered, and I will let folks know your business isn't the caliber they deserve. You can build a better business and leverage barter better by faithfully practicing the Golden Rule.

I believe in a consistent business work ethic. I also understand that cash clients will get first choice on scheduling; we all reserve the premium, high-demand days and times for them.

Every industry has its "slow days". By simply explaining to barter clients that Mondays, Tuesdays and Wednesdays are available to them, we fill in our slow days, keep paying clients happy with the days they most want, and we keep our employees productive all week.

Another practice where we distinguish cash- from barter-clients is when they pay for services. Typically, in the cleaning industry, regular cash customers pay for services at the time of service, on a "pay as you go" system. But, with barter clients, we collect 30 to 90 days of barter 'dollars,' or credits, up front. It helps us reduce the 'pay as you go' bookkeeping on the barter side while maintaining that 'even exchange' of goods or services so important to effective trade.

Finally, we employ our "last minute cancellation fee" policy more firmly with our bartered clients. We tend to overlook or not enforce our policy when cash clients have those last minute cancellations, 'skips' or schedule changes. I am far less inclined to waive that "late cancellation fee" with a barter client. Also, barter clients cannot use a coupon or take advantage of sales and specials. All barters are on our "full retail pricing", but are also never inflated.

The important thing is to establish your rules and practices right up front. In my case, I explain all the parameters, including the fact that "no-notice skips, cancellations, or no-shows" will be considered lost service and will not be refunded. The nonsense we have to tolerate with our precious cash clients is not extended to our barter clients.

Barter Is A Guaranteed Sale

When you are marketing to attract new clients and you've spent hundreds of dollars to get in front of good prospects, they still say "No, thank you" more often than you want. By its very nature, business means a constant search for qualified referrals and new customers. Those hoped-for new customers create profit or fund new business expenses, or enable you to invest in infrastructure.

With barter, however, every purchase you make in trade, every expense you pay for with your goods and services on barter, or investment in infrastructure through barter, is a sale 'Closed' and guaranteed business. Period. You don't "hope for" the new customers to fund those expenditures—they're guaranteed.

If I commit to upgrading my computer system and spend $5,000 on computers, monitors, software and installation, and I ramp up my marketing to help me pay the bill next month when the credit card comes due—what guarantees do I have that I'll be flooded with exactly $10,000 worth of new business—which is what I will need in order to pay that bill when it comes due? Remember, if half of the revenue is spent on my direct labor costs, then I'll need at least $10,000 in new sales to pay the $5,000 credit card bill. That's how we conduct cash business transactions every day…pay cash and pray; spend and hope.

We buy needed equipment or marketing with cash or credit, and then pray like crazy it pays off and the profits will be there to pay the bills on time. What if a terrible storm hits and the phone lines go down the very week your expensive marketing campaign comes out? The campaign that was supposed to generate the revenue to pay for the expenses you added this month? Are the sales guaranteed to come in just because you decided to spend some money on marketing or computer upgrades? Of course not—at least not in the "cash" world.

Just the opposite is true with barter. Even seasoned barterers don't always get this point. *The very act of spending barter credit equals the sale to afford it!* Paying cash for something guarantees you'll be hanging on, hoping you have enough cash flow to make ends meet after the purchase. Buying on trade means you have committed your goods to someone and, in return, they expect to receive your goods. Done deal, no hoping involved. Buying guarantees the selling. For example, I get to provide $5,000 worth of cleaning for the $5,000 worth of computer equipment purchased on barter. The good news for me is I'll clean over time; not all at once. And, my out of pocket expense will only be around $2,500, in direct labor costs; not the $5,000 in cash I would have had to spend in the cash world. This goes a long way towards alleviating that 'pay cash and pray' business malady.

Employee Benefits On Barter

Small companies have a hard time competing for the best employees when it comes to benefits. The benefits of barter can extend far beyond building your business and paying for expenses. Barter can be a powerful tool for creating and providing an employee incentive program or an employee perks program. I've helped maid services all over the world utilize barter as a means to reward their staff and create benefits they couldn't afford otherwise. In addition to having owned a Maid Service for nearly 30 years, I also provide business consulting to service-business owners and my specialty is maid service business consulting. I am always helping small businesses who struggle to compete with the larger companies – the ones with big benefits and big marketing budgets. Barter creates low cost opportunities for companies on a small budget to add benefits for their staff.

Every service business struggles with employee turnover. No matter what the service, the challenge of finding and keeping quality employees can make or break your business. Maid services are notorious for 300% employee turnover, a number I find unacceptable. I don't accept that turnover rate in my own company, nor do I believe others should. Businesses that want to stand out should never accept the "status quo".

Reducing turnover requires knowing how to hire right, train well, equip, motivate, and build loyalty. Barter can help with the "motivate and build loyalty" part. If you are creative, barter can help you add medical and dental benefits, incentives, perks and rewards for your employees that you pay for in bartered goods and services, rather than cash—which you might not have.

I keep a supply of bartered restaurant certificates, massage gift cards, and oil change gift certificates on hand as a way to reward my employees for a 'Job Well Done!' I also use these for the door prizes at Staff Meetings and our Employee Awards Banquets. My business certainly couldn't afford to buy these 'extras' with cash, but I can provide them through barter. I've gifted my employees with tickets to the Ringling Brothers-Barnum & Bailey Circus, Disney On Ice, and a variety of sporting events, which my employees and their families appreciate and enjoy.

When gas prices spiked one summer, all of us were affected. We lost customers, sales dropped and my employees started complaining about the gas prices eating into their budgets. Just another hiccup in the long line of challenging economic conditions for business owners. However, because I keep a large assortment of bartered fast-food certificates on hand, I was able to attach free food certificates with each paycheck all summer long. The free burgers, steak sandwiches, tacos, breakfast sandwiches, and milk shakes from local restaurants helped improve attitudes as we all adjusted to the gas prices.

Another way I've used barter to benefit my employees is to offer a "bonus" using barter. I have a very loyal employee who has worked in my office for years. She never complained about the freeze on raises during some our worst economic struggles, nor the fact that she went without a raise for several years after the events of 9-11, and business was literally "touch-n-go". So, when her daughter got engaged this past year, I told her to get anything she wanted for the wedding through my barter network. She chose the perfect cake and beautiful custom favors that would otherwise have put a big squeeze on her budget. Her cash was freed up for other wedding essentials, her daughter was ecstatic, and I was thrilled to find a meaningful way to tell her and her family how much I appreciated them. The barter 'surpluses' you accrue in the trade associations are money in your pocket without a dime leaving your hand. Beautiful! Candy Haven of Denton, Texas provided outstanding service and a beautiful, delicious cake, all on barter, and with a smile.

You scream, I scream, we all scream for barter! The summer is hot in Texas. Maid services always experience a spike in employee turnover during the hot summer months. Their kids are at home, the houses are harder to clean with other people's kids at home all day, and the heat is so intense tempers flair at the drop of a mop. I decided to use some barter to provide a cool, refreshing treat for my employees in July. The Ben & Jerry's Ice Cream store in Plano, Texas joined my barter association. They were trying to promote their "corporate ice cream sundae parties" so we booked a gig. We scheduled a two-hour, all-you-can-eat ice cream party with all the toppings on payday. We told our employees they could bring their family to our Payday Ice Cream day. It was fun, refreshing, and a welcomed treat on a hot summer day. Something I would not have done if I had to shell out the cash. Talk about employee morale boost—it wasn't the cost, but the thought, that meant so much.

Another great employee perk program, made possible with bartered goodies, was our "no absent" campaign for 90 days. Since absent employees wreck havoc on a maid service and can cost a small fortune in lost business and permanent customer cancellations, we're always looking for perfect attendance incentives. Last summer was particularly rough so we wanted to create a big incentive program this year. We gathered up tons of our bartered certificates and made lovely gifts out of them. We found straw beach bags for $1 and bought several dozen. We put together all kinds of fun incentive gift sets. One beach bag was loaded up with a large beach towel, $1 flip flops, sun screen and a family fun pass to a local water park (purchased on barter); we wrapped it all up in clear cellophane and a bow. The next gift set we created was for a local Mexican food restaurant, certificates purchased on barter of course. We bought corn chips and salsa at the Dollar Store, and giant chip-n-dip bowls on sale at Target Stores for .25 each, and wrapped it all up in cellophane for a fun gift of dinner out! The bartered certificates, all wrapped up as special gifts took on the look and feel of valuable prizes and became the talk of the office for weeks. We also found luxury bath salts, body lotions, and perfumed creams on sale and wrapped those up in cellophane and included the bartered gift certificates for massages and facials—a real treat for women who don't splurge on a lot of pampering. These rewards didn't cost much because the gift-set embellishments were all purchased on clearance, and the bartered certificates were in $25, $50, and $100 increments. The energy and excitement created by a table full of valuable prizes was a powerful incentive to have perfect attendance and was a relatively low-cost employee motivation program. It doesn't mean much to reward someone with $25 for no absences for a month, but give them a chance to take their whole family out for a Mexican food dinner and they'll be motivated and grateful. We've also used barter to reward our top employees. Those high achievers you hope you never have to do without. Yes, I could hand them a $500 bartered voucher for dental work, but instead, we jazzed up that bonus up a little too, to make this "benefit" a little more special. We purchased attractive gift baskets (from The Dollar Store, of course) and lined them with gift basket "grass". We then filled the gift baskets with toothpaste, mouthwash, floss, and breath mints, and popped in the $500 Dental voucher we obtained on barter--wrapping it all up in cellophane and a big bow. Dental insurance is a perk many companies just can't afford. Check with your CPA on how to report this bonus on the employee's W-2 form. The point is, use your barter to build your business: nurture clients, entice prospects, reward employees, and pay your bills. Get a little creative and your barter will go much further.

Since we're talking about creativity, I'll tell you how we gifted up a bunch of oil change gift certificates we got on barter, and used them to attract new clients around Father's Day. We bought inexpensive black plastic tool boxes at Wal-Mart and a few very inexpensive "guy stuff" items to place in the tool boxes (flashlight, bungee cords, tape measure, and duct tape). The entire kit cost lest than $15 to put together. We left the lid open on the kit so all the goodies can be seen, threw in two $30 gift certificates (obtained on barter) for the oil changes, and promoted our "Father's Day Special" which included "$60 worth of oil changes and $500 worth of maid service for 5 chore-free weekends!" A little creativity goes a long way when using barter.

Like Wonder Bread

There is exponential power in barter. It is a practical, dynamic business tool with applications for virtually every business, regardless of size and, like Wonder Bread, barter builds strong businesses 12 ways!

1. **Barter conserves endangered cash.** We never have enough cash to cover what we need so why spend it?
2. **Barter puts staff to work in slow times.** By finding businesses that will take your goods and services in trade, you can keep employees occupied and productive despite slow times of the week or year.
3. **Barter reduces unsold inventory.** When demand slackens, offload idle inventory, unsold office supplies, undercapitalized equipment, overstocked orange t-shirts, empty rooms, unfilled seats, unreserved dining tables, perishable peaches, out-of-style ottomans, languishing lighting, and remnant rugs through barter. There is a better chance of selling at full price through the barter exchange than through traditional, low-profit liquidation.
4. **Barter brings valuable benefits for both parties.** We had an automotive repair service as a client a while back whose business was affected by one of our economic downturns. The owner called to say it was all he could do to pay his mechanics, on which his business relied. He said our service was a luxury he could no longer afford. He was also hundreds of dollars in arrears in payment and we never collected all of it. I didn't understand barter back then and could have offered to trade the balance of what he owed me for auto repairs for

my employees. Too bad I didn't know then what I know now.

5. **Barter generates new cash business.** Usually, the businesses who want to barter don't want to pay cash. You can reap the rewards of positive referrals, however, by putting your best foot forward, and by being attentive, respectful and professional. New markets can be built on barter work.
6. **Barter increases your market.** This is especially true when you use organized barter associations and brokers who open new doors for guaranteed business.
7. **Selection.** Organized barter, especially state, regional or national associations, provide a wider selection of cash-free goods and services from which to choose, unlike private bartering.
8. **Barter lets you support your local economy,** exposing you to other businesses you might not have heard of.
9. **Barter guarantees you** business with barter credit.
10. **Barter generates cash** when you tempt folks with offers they can't resist, that you obtained through barter.
11. **Barter smoothes out** downtimes and off-peak times, strengthening your overall financial condition.
12. **Barter creates,** enhances and develops new professional relationships.

Barter, like yeast, will make your 'dough' rise!

Nothing to Barter?

A friend of mine recently said, "I don't own my own business. I have nothing to barter." She's a business consultant for crying out loud! She's just starting out, which means she's got the perfect product to barter: TIME—and lots of it! It costs her nothing, it will generate testimonials, success stories, and referrals. Hello—she is the perfect candidate for barter. Then she informed me that she owns a vacation home in the mountains, which she only uses a couple times a year. Hello, barter! After a few encouraging words her wheels were spinning.

My sister, Lisa, has worked for Corporate America her entire life. She too, "had nothing to barter." One day she called me up and said, "I found an amazing deal. I'm buying a condo in a popular resort area. It's a foreclosure and a real dog but it's in a prime location. We've got family that can help with some of the remodel, it'll increase in value significantly and we'll all have a condo on the beach to enjoy!" "Awesome", I said, thinking of how I will get to spend a week in her condo, which was within walking distance of the ocean. Then I said, "You know, Lisa, you can get all kinds of work done on barter while you're remodeling."

Weeks later, Lisa told me the tile guy traded his services for two weeks of family vacation, the upholsterer recovered her old couch in trade for a week next summer...and more. Before long the condo was completely remodeled and decorated, and much of it on barter. I'm so proud of her.

Barter isn't just for people who own a business. It's for anyone who owns anything that others consider valuable. Barter is ideal for anyone with surplus time.

My Aunt Betty loved to make quilts. They were entirely hand-stitched, with one-of-a-kind designs she created with stunning fabrics. She'd say they were "therapeutic" for her to make but everyone else said they were breathtaking. If Aunt Betty had charged for her time and skill, those quilts would have cost $1,200, but she was unable to find people who could pay what they were worth. My aunt was living in a small community on a fixed income. Although she might have put her lovely quilts in admiring hands to help her pay for practical needs her community wasn't big enough to do that, unlike the trade exchanges we have today. I believe she would have gotten top dollar in barter if she had taken advantage of this economic currency, affording her many luxuries she did without, like vacations, salon services, carpet cleaning, even dental work. Sadly, my aunt is in hospice today but the Wedding Ring quilt Aunt Betty gave me over 32 years ago is priceless to me. I've used it on every bed we've owned; not a stitch has unraveled, not a piece of fabric has popped up. It's a treasured heirloom. She always wanted to sell them on the retail market, but she couldn't compete with the low prices of machine-stitched quilts, and refused to put all that hard work into them for low compensation. I don't blame her, they were worth much more. She never bartered, she only made them for family gifts, but I believe she could have bartered, and gotten top dollar for her. And who knows, if word got around and her reputation spread, willing cash clients might have followed.

Barter For Start-Ups

New businesses will find barter more profitable than spending cash, especially when trying to establish a name and reputation. Barter builds relationships and word-of-mouth, both of which increase the likelihood of cash paying customers. It also helps you generate testimonials and referrals when paying customers are few and far between. Barter is perfect for a business start up.

When you're starting out there's little cash to spend and never enough customers beating down the door to bring you more. The cash you have on-hand should be saved to pay the bills that can't be bartered like electricity, water, insurance, taxes, and employee wages. For those reasons alone barter makes sense, but there are other advantages, too.

For starters, barter is an incredibly powerful marketing tool. It gets your name out and gets people talking about you. It helps develop relationships you wouldn't have developed otherwise and, if you do a good job while bartering, you'll see more sales, new testimonials and more satisfied customers who will spread the word.

Remember, too, your barter sales are at your full retail price, not the discounted prices we tend to offer when we're hungry for business.

Barter clients keep your staff busy, and it's an excellent way to

> I ordered some very nice custom logo mugs on barter a while back. The logo quality on the mugs was so superior I was happy to order more from her on a cash basis, long after she dropped out of the barter group.

clients are knocking at the doors. Providing a high level of service for cash and barter clients means your staff gains practice, experience, and skills as your business grows.

LET'S MAKE A DEAL!

Being creative, thinking 'outside the box', is one of the keys to growing your business through barter. Remember, your business MUST have incoming cash sales but when you can barter, do. Besides, barter is FUN.

I've sent flowers to people on barter, I've had my carpets and windows cleaned on barter, and I've had my daughter's teeth whitened on barter. I got Lasik surgery on barter. I've spent a summer tanning before a high school reunion, all on barter. And now I'm having facials (on barter) to repair the damage to my skin! It's fun to think of ways to spend my barter and save my cash.

When it comes to barter, the sky's the limit. You are limited only by your own imagination. Every time I buy something now I ask myself, "Could I have bartered for this?" because I hate paying for anything that I could have traded for instead.

I recently met a man who was looking at subleasing some extra office space that I have. When he said he was the general manager of a local steakhouse chain, I asked if he had unlimited dinner certificates. My wheels were spinning but I didn't say anything, I just got his business card. Either he'll call about the office space or I'll call him to see if he wants to trade maid service gift cards for $50 steakhouse gift cards. My employees would love it, and it would be great for a new customer email campaign. I am always thinking about who and how I can barter.

When I need $10,000 in barter credits fast, I'll promote a "Maid Service Gift Card" Special to my barter association members. I invite hundreds of other Association members to purchase $100 gift cards in increments of five. These gift cards are always a popular way to say, 'Thank You' to VIP clients, 'Thinking of you' to friends and family or for their own cleaning needs.

Sometimes I'll put a maximum on my offer, like "only two sets per person," meaning they can buy $500 or $1,000 worth of gift cards. That way, I only need 10 to 20 Association members to purchase the sets, to accrue $10,000 trade credits for that fancy, do-everything copier machine. And, who knows how long it will be before people actually start redeeming those cleaning gift cards, if ever.

Remember, gift cards have an immediate 'Wow!' value for the recipient, but only about 70% are actually redeemed and often not fully redeemed. Some $5 billion (with-a-'B') worth of gift cards went unspent and unredeemed in 2009 in the regular cash market, so barter gift cards and certificates won't all be redeemed either.

Speaking of Gift Cards, you can trade your expiring gift cards. If you're like me, you have a stack of Gift Cards in a drawer somewhere. Ask your prospects and customers to trade their unexpired Gift Cards for your goods or services. We routinely get new customers with our "Gift Card Swap" Program. First, we invite customers to trade their expiring gift cards for our maid service gift cards. They get rid of gift cards they won't use, and we get a chance a winning a new customer. It's a perfect trade. Now that they've tried us, we've attracted a new customer who is a candidate for repeat service. Most of the folks who take us up on our 'swap cards for services' might not have tried us otherwise. The gift card swap gives them a reason to give us a try, we get a gift we can pass along to employees or use in our next email campaign, and they find out what a treat it is to come home to a clean house. What a deal for everyone, just a creative trade.

SAY "I DO!" TO BARTER

It just might be possible to say the crown jewel of my bartering stories was picking up the phone when a writer from *Modern Bride Magazine* called me for an interview. She'd read one of my business blogs, where I talked all about the wedding we had for my daughter, almost entirely on barter. I couldn't have asked for better press than a national magazine mentioning my consulting and barter smarts. Talk about free, national exposure for a concept I was passionate about. The real story of what we were able to accomplish for Amy's wedding was even more fun than the article that followed.

When Amy (my baby) and John got engaged, we were thrilled. I, of course, wanted to give my daughter her dream wedding. My husband wanted to pay cash so we didn't end up like a lot of people do, ringing up a fortune in credit card debt for a one-day event. My husband and I agreed on a small cash budget and I negotiated the rest on barter.

My daughter wanted a Sunday afternoon wedding, which proved to make it easier to find prospective barter partners. Sunday is a light day to work with after the traditional Saturday wedding crush. I can tell you, we probably would not have been able to schedule the photographer, the photo booth for the Reception or the Limo on barter, if the wedding had been on a Friday or a Saturday. Little compromises amount to huge savings when it comes to barter.

My search for a photographer was critical. I didn't want to settle for a newbie who was starved for work and might not have the expertise I wanted, so I interviewed several and found one who was busy enough to prove to me she was a pro and flexible enough to barter for the Sunday we had on the calendar.

The photographer did an amazing job on the pre-wedding portraits and an outstanding job of wedding photos. We love the photo album and picture CD, and I've already referred her to three new (cash) customers. She still hasn't redeemed her $2,600 worth of cleanings - they've been remodeling – but, when she's ready, my company will do a $100 cleaning every other week for a year. And, if she's never ready, I can give her twenty-six $100 maid service gift cards that she can use to close some big photography deals or give away as baby shower gifts, or whatever. Just imagine offering the Mother of the Bride a $300 maid service gift card special to help win the bid of a really big gig. Either way, whether she ever redeems the barter or not, we have beautiful wedding pictures that I didn't have to shell out the cash to get.

We also managed to get the most beautiful cake I'd ever seen on barter. The cake tasting, at Candy Haven in Denton was fun and memorable. We took pictures and videos and Amy chose the Italian Cream, of course. All the flowers, strings of orchids for the outside ceremony, boutonnieres, corsages and the bridal bouquet were just what Amy wanted and beautifully fresh, and ordered on barter. The photo booth, allowing guests to 'capture the moment,' was novel, fun and cash-free. The elegant Limo that swept Amy and John off on their Honeymoon was the Happy Ending to our beautiful day and the finishing touch of a day full of bartered services. Why write a check or pay cash when barter will do?

The Perils And Pitfalls Of Barter

We've talked at length about staying 'even,' in barter exchanges. But be careful, when you're looking at what's available for barter not to pay more than fair market value for items you receive on barter. I wouldn't pay double for something in the cash world and I refuse to pay double for anything on barter. If your margins are around 50% like mine, paying double what something is worth can undue all of the savings. Let's talk about some examples of when I've just said "No!"

I really, really want granite counter tops for my kitchen. Someone in my trade exchange barters custom concrete counter tops that he says are, "as pretty as granite." I invited this "artist" out for a quote. He measured and shared all the reasons why his concrete work of art was superior to granite. Then he gave us a quote. It was absurd. One I am certain he would never have quoted a prospective cash customer. Then, he added insult to injury by saying, "And I will do this on half cash, half barter." We told him to take a hike. Vendors like that don't belong in the barter group and shouldn't be allowed to remain as a member when they are caught pulling these stunts.

Another time, I called a very popular advertiser in my barter exchange group. His account is managed by another broker who permits the 50-50 cash-barter arrangements which jeopardizes the stability of the entire trade exchange. I told the advertiser I was only interested in 100% barter and he assured me that was his desire as well, so we set up an appointment to meet. After a 30 minute presentation of all the benefits of his product and services, I was more excited than ever to do business with him.

That is, until he presented me with the "sucker price" and terms of a 50-50 cash-barter arrangement. What? I reminded him of our earlier conversation, about 100% barter, and that I clearly communicated my expectations before making the appointment. He wasted my time. Not only did he quote me a price for advertising that was about 25% higher than his regular cash customers would pay, he also wanted 50% cash, and 50% on trade.

A more desperate member in need of advertising in this high-end medium might have said yes to his offer. After all, 50-50 can be better than paying 100% cash for something you really want. But he inflated the price as well. His argument was his margins were too high, which prevented him from being able to offer his services at 100% trade. My answer to him was "Then you should get out of the trade group; that's not how it works and you are hurting the overall reputation of the organization." I refuse to barter with people inside the trade associations that violate the rules. If more people refused to barter with him he would either drop out or comply like the rest of us. I really wanted to use his advertising, but I just had to say "no".

I believe in playing by the rules: I chose this particular barter association because I want 100% barter and I appreciate the association and its individual members for protecting the integrity of the 100% barter system. The best organizations police their members to insure all are trading fair and 100%. The "50-50" barters (half cash, half trade) are not allowed and threaten the stability of the entire program when not enforced. When trade members get frustrated because everyone in the organization is inflating prices or demanding half in cash, the barter economy crumbles.

Lessons from My Broker, Gary Smith

"Debbie Sardone's experience with barter and its contribution to her business' success has gotten my attention. Surely, you too are seeing new ways to improve your balance sheet, explore new markets, reduce cash outlays and propel your business.

Debbie asked me to give you an 'insider's' point of view, as a seasoned trade association broker and ITEX franchise owner. ITEX is the largest trade association in North America but there are hundreds more throughout the world, each with their own policies and procedures. So, while I hope you will be inclined to join ITEX at some point, you owe it to yourself to do the research on the trade associations available to you. One of the first things you'll want to consider is what goods or services you want to barter for. Maid service businesses like Debbie's barter for employee uniforms, employee benefits, advertising space, banners, carpet cleaning, a plumber and more. Perhaps you could use tickets to local entertainment and sporting events for employees or customers, fleet maintenance or cleaning services. Will local trading suffice, or are you interested in national or international options? In order to handle trading across country and around the world, trade associations, including ITEX, use a trade 'draft.' Each member has his or her own separate account, much like a bank account. When a member sells goods or service to another member, the 'Seller's' ITEX account is paid – or credited – and the buyer's account is debited. Whether buying or selling within the vast market of 'merchandise' available, it is the trade 'balance' in your account that determines how much you can 'purchase' at any given time. Private trade (called "direct trade") means if you want fleet auto repairs from 'Bill's

Auto Shop,' you and Bill are the only ones who can barter. Trades within a trade association, on the other hand, enable you to spend your trade drafts or credits anywhere, with anyone in the trade association. If you and Bill are members of the same association, you can use your barter account to pay Bill for fleet service. He, however, has the freedom to use his account to buy what he needs and wants from anyone, anywhere in the entire organization. At ITEX, with more than 24,000 members, he'd have endless choices. Suppose your maid service and a lawyer propose a direct trade: $1,000 of legal services in exchange for $1,000 worth of cleaning services agreed to with a handshake. Six months later, you have provided $1,000 worth of cleaning services but the lawyer has been swamped and has only just begun addressing your legal work. Then, suddenly, he dies. You're left with no recourse. A vital element of organized barter is the protection of your trade dollars. In organized barter, the attorney's trade account would have been debited immediately for your cleaning services and your account credited, with recourse from the organization if something unforeseen happened to your barter-provider. And, as opposed to direct barter, you are free to use your organized barter account when and where you need it, not necessarily on the attorney for whom you clean. The point is, no matter what happens to you or the other association member, the trade association protects your investment. Imagine if your business needs weren't restricted by proximity to your business. What if a list or directory of goods and services sparked ideas you'd never considered? Or provided more vendors, with more specialties, skills or resources than those around you? By providing you with more resources, a trade organization can help you strengthen and build your business. Imagine being able to barter for Pittsburgh Steelers tickets for your Dad in Pensacola, a new water heater for your daughter's home in New Jersey, or silk-screened t-shirts for the staff, all without missing a beat. Barter like this doesn't happen locally in direct barter. Direct trade limits you in a way trade associations don't. You can be a 'Big Thinker' barterer and run a strong, stable business. Whether you are doing a direct trade or trading through a trade association, trade "value" should be established at the retail value of the items being traded. If your maid service offers cleaning with a retail value of $200 per cleaning, and you're trading for printing of business cards that cost only $50, that's not an even trade. Because trade exchanges use a common currency, this problem never arises. In the example above, the printer's trade account is debited 200 'trade dollars' for the value of the maid service while your account is debited 50 'trade dollars,' the cost of the business cards. You each are credited or debited for the actual value of your services provided. In trade, just as with cash, the market determines fair market value and if a trade association member overcharges, other trade exchange members will trade elsewhere. Hopefully, they will also report the member to the trade association for over-charging, and he or she will either reduce the price to market value or be asked to leave the association. Accounting is a standard business practice that enables business owners to monitor their company's strengths and weaknesses on paper. Enacted by Congress, in 1982, the Internal Revenue Service enforces the tracking and accounting of barter activities as a business requirement. For accounting purposes, trades are business activities that result in income or expenses. Trade associations provide their members with an itemized accounting at the end of each billing cycle, whether monthly or quarterly, which helps your tax professional determine income, fees, business-related expenses (tax deductible), etc. A trade association does everything possible to minimize the time its members spend tallying barter income and expenses. And, as you can imagine, association members that are CPAs or other tax professionals, are available to you, on barter, to prepare your taxes for you, freeing up the cash you may be paying someone locally. If you do several direct trades with different businesses, keeping track of those trades will be a major challenge. While you may believe, "I did $500 worth of maid service for Tom, but I've only used $125 worth of his product, so my balance is $375," Tom may be thinking, "Sharon has $225 worth of my product." You can see how likely it is for direct barter to get complicated between you and Tom. If you are also doing direct barter with Joe, Mary, Bill and Susan, it takes detailed records, good communications and unusually gracious folks to all feel they are walking away with an equal share of what they individually invested. Eliminate the complications by using an association of organized barter. Members' accounts are credited in full immediately when they provide products or services and charged in full when they buy. Why complicate life when there's a proven, easier way?"

Gary Smith, ITEX of Lewisville, Texas

Which Trade Exchange Association?

Now, more than ever, you're aware that private trade is both limited and risky but which trade exchange is best for you?

There are three types of exchange associations available today, all of which offer centralized membership services and a trade currency exclusive to their membership. The first type of exchange is a 'local' exchange association open to businesses within a certain community or metropolitan area. As a rule, these associations have a smaller number of members and, therefore, more limited number of trade opportunities. The second type of exchange is the 'regional' trade exchange offering organized accounting and membership services within a specific geographic area. The third type of exchange is a 'national/international' exchange association. ITEX falls into this category. Geographically, it offers memberships to businesses across the country and the world. Members of a National/International trade association are free to trade with any member, regardless of their geographic location. Such exchange associations have the highest number of members in the barter industry and offer the widest variety and breadth of barter opportunities. Additionally, they provide a competitive edge to members by having branch offices serving the major metropolitan areas. ITEX, for example, has approximately 100 'local' branch offices serving its members across the United Sates, Canada and the Caribbean. ITEX members benefit from a 'world' of goods and services as much as the convenience and attention of a dedicated, local office. Not all of the larger exchanges have branch or satellite offices. Some provide centralized, Internet or Call Center trade floors and all transactions are handled on-line or by phone. While this type of processing is part of today's way of doing business, it lacks that personal attention so many of us have come to value with 'membership.'

Membership Has It Privileges

Yes, there is a cost to be a member. The trade exchange brokers are offering and delivering a tremendous service to the business-members. What you will find, though, is that most trade exchanges deliver a lot of benefits for very little cost. When it comes to fees, trade exchanges will vary from organization to organization. You may find an exchange with fees that are next to nothing. Their fees are so low in fact you may wonder how they can stay in business. It's easy…they don't! Some disappear - usually without warning - very soon. With your trade exchange, you should not only expect to pay reasonable fees, you should make sure of it. Below I will discuss some common types of fees. Just remember - you get what you pay for. Sometimes, the best deal is *not* the cheapest deal.

The first fee is the "Membership" or "Initial" fee. This could be minimal or it could be well over $1,000 in cash. Currently ITEX has no "Initial" fee if you are on auto-pay. Another fee is the "monthly", "accounting" or "association" fee. This is typically a recurring fee charged each billing period. It can vary from "no charge" to $30 each billing cycle. Generally, this fee simply helps to offset administrative type expenses, such as mailing statements to members, and helps defray some of the payroll expense. Where trade exchanges really generate the income to stay in business, is through 'transaction' fees.

A sale and a purchase are each transactions. Some exchanges charge a fee on both the sale and the purchase; some charge a fee only on the purchase. The amount of the transaction fee is typically based on a percentage of the transaction value and is often 5% - 8% on the sale, 5% - 8% on the purchase, 10% on the purchase only, or some combination thereof. Generally speaking, transaction fees usually total between 10% and 20% in cash and this, as well as all other fees, vary from association to association. Word to the wise: find out what fees are involved.

Be certain to weigh all the fees against the size of the association and member services offered. If you think it's a fair price for the opportunities, then I encourage you to join.

A Last Word

There is no single more powerful business tool than barter. It opens new markets and generates new sales and income. It can increase your profit margin and your cash on-hand. How much, you ask? It depends on how much you barter. Organized barter is here to stay. The continuing growth of associations demonstrates the profound value they provide to businesses everywhere. May your business profit from barter as well.

Testimonials

"Debbie, You taught me everything I know about barter! Thank you, I have learned so much."
SP – New York

"Let me start by saying that the information you share is INVALUABE! There is no one else out there like you who is willing to help...not even my Franchise! I cannot even express how much you've helped me......you have saved my business, truly! I was ready to sell. You gave me the inner-strength to believe that I CAN do it!"
CK – Florida

"I want you to know that I am implementing your program 100%; all the way. There's nothing like your program out there! I know I'll be successful if I follow your guidance."
LB – Pennsylvania

"You are already getting me off to a more profitable business and that excites me! Thank you for your time and sacrifice to help others like myself."
OJ – Missouri

"A Big Thank You! I have realized I am not a bad business woman, just the opposite. You have helped me get back my confidence and my relentless energy for the business I love."
LB – Ohio

Resources

For more information regarding the barter industry, or to find directories of local, national, and international trade exchanges, go to: http://www.nate.org/ and http://www.irta.com/

Check out these sites for great local barter resources: www.craigslist.org/

www.barterquest.com

www.barterbuys.com

For information on two of the largest national trade associations in the United States, go to: www.itex.com and www.imsbarter.com

For more information regarding barter and your taxes, go to: http://www.irs.gov/businesses/small/article/0,,id=113437,00.html

To learn more about recent changes in the barter industry, and how barter can improve your company's bottom line, go to *Barter News* magazine, at: www.barternews.com

Or, read informative articles regarding barter, at: www.entrepreneur.com

ABOUT THE AUTHOR

Debbie Sardone knew how to make a buck long before she discovered the secret to hanging on to it. Now a tried-and-true barter advocate, she is sometimes referred to as a 'Barter-preneur' because of her ability to turn good ideas into successful business enterprises with the help of barter.

Owner of *Buckets & Bows Maid Service*, and KYSO consulting (a service business consultancy firm) Debbie provides expert coaching to cleaning industry business owners. Debbie is also founder of the national non-profit *Cleaning For A Reason*, which provides free housecleaning services to women with cancer. A popular speaker and author, Sardone practices what she preaches and has bartered thousands of dollars in goods and services over the last ten years, saving herself and her businesses a small fortune in cash, credit, and advertising costs!

A 30 year veteran of the residential cleaning industry, Sardone's business savvy, experience and intuitive grasp of universal business truths have helped hundreds of other business owners experience the joy of entrepreneurial success.

Debbie is frequently featured on national and regional television, including NBC Nightly News, KTVT – TV Channel 11, WFAA – TV Channel 8 and Fox4News – KDFW, for her work with the *Cleaning For A Reason* Foundation. Her ingenuity, energy, entrepreneurial expertise and successes have also brought Debbie recognition and interviews by a broad spectrum of well-known publications, including CNN MONEY (October 2008), PROFITS Magazine, CM Management Magazine, Modern Bride (July 2007), Ladies Home Journal (April 2010) and more.